W9-DAE-924

WITHDRAWN

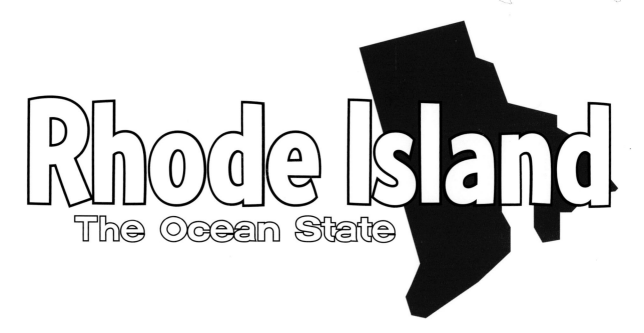

Rhode Island
The Ocean State

Robin Koontz

Huntington City
Township Public Library
255 West Park Drive
Huntington, IN 46750

PowerKiDS
press™

New York

Published in 2011 by The Rosen Publishing Group, Inc.
29 East 21st Street, New York, NY 10010

Copyright © 2011 by The Rosen Publishing Group, Inc.

All rights reserved. No part of this book may be reproduced in any form without permission in writing from the publisher, except by a reviewer.

First Edition

Editor: Amelie von Zumbusch
Book Design: Greg Tucker
Layout Design: Ashley Burrell
Photo Researcher: Jessica Gerweck

Photo Credits: Cover, pp. 13, 17, 22 (tree, bird) Shutterstock.com; p. 5 © www.iStockphoto.com/Myles Dumas; p. 7 Stock Montage/Hulton Archive/Getty Images; p. 9 © North Wind Picture Archives; p. 11 William K. Daby/Getty Images; p. 15 © David H. Wells/age fotostock; p. 19 Travel Ink/Getty Images; p. 22 (fish) © www.iStockphoto.com/Emmgunn; p. 22 (flower) © www.iStockphoto.com/Constance McGuire; p. 22 (Nathanael Greene) MPI/Stringer/Getty Images; p. 22 (Gilbert Stuart) Wikimedia Commons; p. 22 (Meredith Vieira) Mark Von Holden/Getty Images.

Library of Congress Cataloging-in-Publication Data

Koontz, Robin Michal.
  Rhode Island : the Ocean State / Robin Koontz. — 1st ed.
      p. cm. — (Our amazing states)
  Includes index.
  ISBN 978-1-4488-0650-8 (library binding) — ISBN 978-1-4488-0732-1 (pbk.) — ISBN 978-1-4488-0733-8 (6-pack)
  1. Rhode Island—Juvenile literature. I. Title.
  F79.3.K66 2011
  974.5—dc22
                                              2009050868

Manufactured in the United States of America

CPSIA Compliance Information: Batch #WS10PK: For Further Information contact Rosen Publishing, New York, New York at 1-800-237-9932

Contents

The Smallest State

Rhode Island is the smallest state in the United States. Many people call it Little Rhody because it is so small. Rhode Island is also known as the Ocean State. The Atlantic Ocean lies south of Rhode Island. Many of the state's towns and cities are on a part of the ocean called Narragansett Bay. There are more than 30 islands in the bay. The state has almost 400 miles (644 km) of beaches.

Rhode Island is part of New England. New England is a group of states in the northeastern United States. Its beautiful beaches make Rhode Island a great place to vacation. People visit old houses there, too. Rhode Island is known for its history.

The city of Newport, Rhode Island, is on Aquidneck Island, in Narragansett Bay. Visitors to Newport can see many historic buildings and enjoy the bay's natural beauty.

Friendly Neighbors

Rhode Island's Narragansett Bay area was home to many Native Americans. They lived there for thousands of years before anyone else came. Many of the Indians had two homes. One was called a longhouse. Families would share a longhouse during the winter. In summer, the Indians lived in houses called wigwams.

In the 1600s, English **colonists** arrived. Roger Williams founded the first English settlement. He came from nearby Massachusetts. He left because people there did not agree with his beliefs. Williams got along well with the native people. The Narragansett Indians sold land to him in 1636. The settlement that he founded there is now the city of Providence, Rhode Island.

In October 1635, Roger Williams (right) was asked to leave Massachusetts. By that point, he was friendly with the Narragansetts so he went to them for help and land.

The Fight for Freedom

Soon, other English people founded settlements on Narragansett Bay. The settlers agreed to form one community. In 1663, the king of England officially **united** the settlements into one colony.

By the 1770s, the people of Rhode Island and 12 other colonies wanted to break away from England. The colonists fought a war with England and won. The colonies became states. The states came together to form the United States of America. The leaders of this new country wrote a set of laws called the Constitution. Rhode Island was the last of the 13 states to agree to the Constitution. Rhode Islanders would accept it only after the Bill of Rights was added. This part of the Constitution guards certain freedoms.

Anne Hutchinson (center) came to Rhode Island after she was forced out of Massachusetts because of her beliefs. She helped found Portsmouth, one of Rhode Island's first settlements.

Islands and Hills

Rhode Island is small, but it has lots of islands. Block Island is the farthest off the coast. Lots of people take vacations there. Many of the state's islands are in Narragansett Bay. The biggest of these is Aquidneck Island. The smallest is Whale Rock. It is shaped like the back of a whale.

The northern and western parts of Rhode Island are called the Western Rocky Upland. This part of the state has rocky hills and forests. There are rivers, ponds, and small lakes there, too.

As many places near oceans do, Rhode Island has mild weather. It is not too hot there in the summer. Winters do not get very cold.

Rhode Island's Western Rocky Upland has lots of stone walls. In the past, farmers pulled the stones out of the ground to clear fields to grow crops. Then, they built walls with the stones.

What Lives in Rhode Island?

Trees cover more than three-fifths of Rhode Island. Some of these trees are hardwoods, such as oaks and maples. They have colorful leaves in the fall. Rhode Island also has evergreens, such as spruces, hemlocks, and pines. These trees stay green all year.

Animals, such as raccoons, rabbits, squirrels, and owls, live in the state's forests. Rhode Island's islands and beaches are home to many shorebirds. Gulls, terns, and loons all live there.

The best-known Rhode Island bird is likely a chicken! Rhode Island Reds were first bred in Little Compton, Rhode Island. This kind of chicken was named the state bird in 1954. It is now one of the most **popular** chickens in the world.

Rhode Island Reds, such as this bird, are raised for both their meat and their eggs. Rhode Island Red hens lay brown eggs. They are known for being dependable egg layers.

Farm to Factory

The Blackstone River valley runs through northeastern Rhode Island. It is known as the Birthplace of the American **Industrial Revolution**. In 1793, people there built the first American mill for making cloth. Pawtucket, Rhode Island, had many early tool and machine makers, too. Soon, more mills were built. Cities grew up quickly.

Today, Rhode Island has factories that make things such as **jewelry**, silverware, and lightbulbs. Medical supplies and parts for computers are also made there. Businesses such as **insurance** and health care companies are a big part of Rhode Island's **economy**, too. People in Rhode Island also catch and sell fish, lobsters, and **scallops**. Farmers sell fruit, eggs, vegetables, and flowers.

These Rhode Islanders are quahoggers. That means that they catch shellfish called quahogs for a living. Quahogs are a kind of clam.

Welcome to Providence

Providence is the capital of Rhode Island. It is also the state's biggest city. Art is a big part of life in Providence. The Rhode Island School of Design is there.

Some people visit Providence to learn about its rich history. Visitors can walk the Mile of History on Benefit Street. They can see buildings there from different points in the city's history. Visitors who like history can also ride on the Crescent Park Carousel. It was built in 1895. It is all that is left of an old **amusement park**.

Visitors also love to see the Big Blue Bug in Providence. It is a giant fake termite. It is more than 900 times bigger than a real termite!

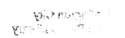

These people are ice-skating at a skating rink in downtown Providence. There are lots of fun things to do in Providence.

Huntington City
Township Public Library

Seaside Wonder

The beautiful city of Newport, Rhode Island, draws many visitors. The city is on Aquidneck Island. In the summer, Newport has music **festivals**. Its harbor is full of boats. Sailing races often take place there.

Newport has a long history. It was founded in 1639. In 1763, Jewish settlers built Touro **Synagogue** there. It is the oldest synagogue in the United States. Visitors can learn a lot about the history of the U.S. Navy at the city's Naval War College Museum.

In the 1800s, many rich families built huge summer homes in Newport. The Newport Cliff Walk winds along the shoreline there. People can enjoy the beautiful views and see some of the big houses.

The Breakers is one of the biggest summer homes in Newport. It has more than 70 rooms. Its look is based on Italian palaces from the sixteenth century.

Rhode Island is home to people from around the world. You can taste foods from many different countries there. You can also eat some special Rhode Island foods. Cornmeal pancakes, called johnnycakes, are one popular Rhode Island food.

There are lots of ways to enjoy the outdoors in Rhode Island. The state has many bicycle trails and hiking trails. People walk on the long, sandy beaches. There are many lighthouses to see. Bird-watching is popular in Rhode Island, too. Block Island has a big wildlife **refuge**. This land is set aside for wild animals. Visitors there can see many birds, rolling hills, and views of the ocean. There are so many reasons to love Rhode Island!

Glossary

amusement park (uh-MYOOZ-ment PAHRK) A place with rides, games, and other fun things to do.

colonists (KAH-luh-nists) People who move to a new place but are still ruled by the leaders of the country from which they came.

economy (ih-KAH-nuh-mee) The way in which a government oversees its goods and services.

festivals (FES-tih-vulz) Special times of parties and feasting.

Industrial Revolution (in-DUS-tree-ul reh-vuh-LOO-shun) A time in history beginning in the mid-1700s, when power-driven machines were first used to produce goods in large numbers.

insurance (in-SHUR-ints) Protection against loss or harm.

jewelry (JOO-ul-ree) Objects worn on the body that are made of special metals, such as gold and silver, and valued stones.

popular (PAH-pyuh-lur) Liked by lots of people.

refuge (REH-fyooj) A place where something is kept safe.

scallops (SKAH-lups) A kind of shellfish.

synagogue (SIH-nih-gog) A temple or a house of prayer for Jewish people.

united (yoo-NYT-ed) Brought together to act as a single group.

Rhode Island State Symbols

State Tree
Red Maple

State Fish
Striped Bass

State Flag

State Bird
Rhode Island Red

State Flower
Violet

State Seal

Famous People from Rhode Island

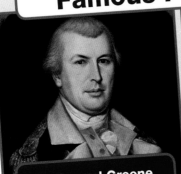
Nathanael Greene
(1742–1786)
Born in Warwick, RI
Revolutionary War
General

Gilbert Stuart
(1755–1828)
Born in Saunderstown, RI
Artist

Meredith Vieira
(1953–)
Born in Providence, RI
TV Show Host

22

Rhode Island State Map

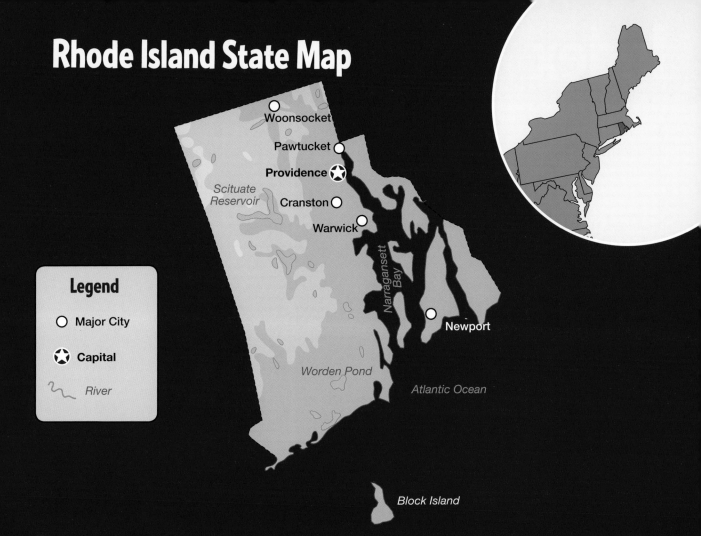

Woonsocket

Pawtucket

Providence

Scituate
Reservoir

Cranston

Warwick

Narragansett
Bay

Newport

Legend

○ Major City

★ Capital

〰 River

Worden Pond

Atlantic Ocean

Block Island

Rhode Island State Facts

Population: About 1,048,319

Area: 1,212 square miles (3,139 sq km)

Motto: "Hope"

Song: "Rhode Island's It for Me," words by Charlie Hull and music by Maria Day

Index

A
amusement park, 16
Atlantic Ocean, 4

B
beaches, 4, 12, 20
businesses, 14

C
chicken(s), 12
cities, 4, 6, 14, 16, 18
colonists, 6, 8

E
economy, 14

F
festivals, 18

H
history, 4, 16, 18
home(s), 6, 12, 18, 20

I
Industrial Revolution, 14
island(s), 4, 10, 12, 18,
    20

J
jewelry, 14

K
king, 8

L
Little Rhody, 4
longhouse, 6

N
Narragansett Bay, 4, 6,
    8, 10
Native Americans, 6
New England, 4

P
part(s), 4, 8, 10, 14, 16

R
refuge, 20

S
scallops, 14

T
Touro Synagogue, 18
towns, 4

Web Sites

Due to the changing nature of Internet links, PowerKids Press has developed an online list of Web sites related to the subject of this book. This site is updated regularly. Please use this link to access the list:

www.powerkidslinks.com/amst/ri/

24